T0195832

THERESA'S TREASURES

Theresa Rosemary Lawson

WestBow Press books may be ordered through booksellers or by contacting:

WestBow Press
A Division of Thomas Nelson & Zondervan
1663 Liberty Drive
Bloomington, IN 47403
www.westbowpress.com
844-714-3454

Scripture taken from the King James Version of the Bible.

ISBN: 978-1-6642-6932-3 (sc)
ISBN: 978-1-6642-6933-0 (e)

Library of Congress Control Number: 2022911296

Print information available on the last page.

WestBow Press rev. date: 06/17/2022

THERESA'S TREASURES

CONTENTS

WHAT IS YOUR DREAM

Do you want to be a teacher
Do you want to fly a kite
Do you want to see the moon
Are you ready to take the flight
Just open a book
You'll be right there
Your mind will think it
Your heart will be there
Now close your eyes and dream a dream
And ask God to make it all come true
He sees you
He hears you
He knows who you are
Just believe and trust Jesus
And all will be fine
You won't have to worry
God will work
In His time

MEMORIES

Let me think
What did I think
When I was only three
Did I think of fairy tales or did I think of Thee
It was You, O Lord
I needed then
More than anyone else
You were not pleased with certain things
That were not my fault
You loved me then
You love me now
O praise your name for that
You brought me through those unsure years
And gave me faith in You

INNOCENT

Wonderful baby
Loved with my heart
Never to be taken
From me
Please don't depart
You are so precious
Precious to me
Precious to Jesus
Precious to thee
Sweet and tender
Nice and new
I am sorry my angel
I am sorry for me
I am glad for you

HEAVEN

Heaven is the place to be
Where one would love to spend eternity
There's a street of gold and pearly gates
There is no sorrow there
There is no hate
God is there
And God is Love
No place on earth
Can compare to this
Just think of it
Eternal bliss
Heaven is His reward for me
Is it for you
Heaven is the place to be
I've found my niche
I've found it here
Where Jesus is
And there is no fear

DO YOU KNOW

What's right
What's wrong
Who's right
Who's wrong
This one thing that I perceive
The King James Bible is right
That's what
God, my Jesus
He's who
He is right
All the time
Every time

TRUE RICHES

What is it to be rich
What is it to be poor
Well I have Jesus, now that's rich
You see, Jesus is God, and God is Love
And He owns everything, anyway
Someone has said,
"You have to know someone in this life."
Well that's certainly true for the next life
To have a place in Heaven
You have to have Jesus
He is the only One
So then, why keep wasting time
On what is not important
Remember every second counts
Also remember you can only have true riches when
You know Christ Jesus the Lord
For in Him, you will find treasure like no other
Truly, you will
Like as in the King James Bible, as in Psalms 34:8
"O taste and see that the Lord is good:
Blessed is the man that trusteth in Him."
True riches = The Word of God
The King James Bible
Read it everyday and be rich

WEALTHY PLACE

I am in a wealthy place
I am in God's grace
I am blessed
Worthy is His Holy name
Yesterday, today, forever
He is the same
Jesus Christ, my Lord
He's the absolute best
Richer than the richest man
I receive all from His hand
I am blessed
I share with you my wealth
My favorite verse from the King James Bible:
Il Corinthians 12:9
"And He saith unto me,
My grace is sufficient for thee:
For my strength is made perfect in weakness.
Most gladly, therefore, will I rather glory in my
Infirmities,
That the power of Christ may rest upon me."

TRUE BREAD

Feed me with food.
That is satisfying to me.
True Bread.
The Bread of Life.
Fill me up.
Restore me.
Revive me.
Give me life.
I am hungry.
Feed me.
My spirit yearns for Thee.
To know Thee.
To cherish and obey Thee.
When I am full.
Then will I praise Thee.
O Lord of my life.
Your Word is my daily bread.
It sustains me It comforts me.
Like no ordinary food can.
Because it is the True Bread.
The Word of God.
The King James Bible.

SECRET THINGS

I am I
And you are you
I am not in this world to please you
Except for your edification
But my purpose
is to please
The Almighty One
The King of Kings
And Lord of Lords
Precisely
For, you see
He made me for Himself and His good pleasure
Therefore, I obey Him
Because that is what pleases Him most
So when He tells me to
"Go ye therefore and teach all nations
Baptizing them in the name of the Father
And of the Son, and of the Holy Ghost"
I go
He is with me always and forever
He will never leave me
He has promised me
Therefore
I believe
I trust

TRUE TREASURE

I am a soulwinner for Jesus
To this end am I come
Therefore, wherever He leads me, I go
I open my mouth, He speaks through me, I speak the truth in love
For there is no greater message
I certainly have my flaws, but oh my
He is perfect and His message is divine
Therefore, I am standing on the promises of Christ, my Saviour
Such as, in the King James Bible, it says:
"Lo, I am with thee always, even until the end of the world. Amen."
"l will never leave thee, nor forsake thee."
"l am He that calleth thee and will also do it,"
"Ask and ye shall receive, that your joy may be full."
"Call unto me, and I will answer thee, and shew thee,
Great and mighty things which thou knowest not."
"Trust in the Lord, with all thine heart,
And lean not unto thine own understanding,
In all thy ways, acknowledge Him, and He shall direct thy paths."
"Greater love hath no man, than this, that a man
lay down his life for his friends."
Try listening to some favorite hymns of the faith, like as:
I am come to the garden with Him, also :
The old account was settled long ago.
My mother's favorite too (How great thou art!)
Better yet, sing them
Just so you know, my mother is in Heaven with Her Saviour whom she loves.
Praise the Lord!

TRUE VICTORY

True victory comes from
The power of Jesus' blood
It is all or nothing
Either He saves or not
It is no gamble
God covers me and my sin
In His precious blood
He remembers my sin no more
Thus, you should not
Remember my sin no more
But, remember this
The gospel message
Give it out, with a shout
Praise the Lord!

TRUE PROFESSION

You are the One
I've been waiting for
You are the One
I truly adore
You are the One
I want
And
Only You
And
No more
Let my ears hear
Your Word
Lord
Let my eyes see
You
In everyone I meet
Let me touch the hem of your garment Lord
That I may be whole
Let me taste and see how good
You really are Lord
Let me smell Your fragrance wherever I am
Let me say and do all that you want me to
Let me please You

Printed in the United States
by Baker & Taylor Publisher Services